What They Are Saying About *Shine On!*

Angel Marie's book Shine On! is a must-read for anyone who wants to stand up, stand out, and shine. Her action-packed tips, tools, and ideas can help you shine with confidence, enthusiasm, and courage in all areas of your life!
—Julie Carrier, Emmy Nominee, Award-winning National Speaker and Author of *BeYOUtiful,* and Founder of BeYOUtifulClub.com

Shine On! answers and solves the problems facing our modern generation by simplifying the confusing complexities facing all generations and clearly delineates workable solutions and applications. Kudos, Angel Marie. You rock!
—DJ Khamis, International Artist,
Board of Directors of The Stars Foundation UN/UNICEF

Angel's message, "Shine On" is one that has helped me excel in business and pageantry. While I competed in the United States pageant, my focus was to not only let my light shine but also to remind my pageant sisters to shine their light as well. I truly believe that is why I was honored with the award of Miss Congeniality.
—Christina Wagner, Ms. Woman Arizona United States 2016,
 President, Your Business Ambassador

Shine On! definitely inspired me to get my "Shine on!" Great message. Bottom line: this book rocks!
—Craig Duswalt, Speaker, Author, Radio Host, and
Creator of Rockstar Marketing (www.craigduswalt.com)

Angel Marie's message offers amazing insights on how to shift attitude and perspective to create more joy! Take it from someone who's lived life—Angel Marie knows her stuff! This book is a life-changer!
—Chris Warner, Actor, Speaker, Coach, Consultant

I love the Shine On! message... This is a great book to help motivate you every day to be your best!
—Travis Brown, International Speaker, Best-selling Author, TV Celebrity

Angel Marie truly shines in her message! It's a thoughtful and practical guide to self-esteem and happiness.
—Lea Woodford, TV/Radio Personality and Publisher of *SmartFem Magazine*

We had a great event with Angel Marie. She brought us a professional, effective, and unique experience. Angel Marie's Shine On! message is something different and engaging for the kids. Actually, her message is what everybody needs to hear.
—Sarah Johnson, Stage Manager, Reading for Freedom

A fabulous message for everyone! Incorporating quotes, stories, and action steps to spark your imagination and show you how to accomplish success in life!
—Jill Lublin, 3-time Best-selling Author and International Speaker (PublicityCrashCourse.com/FreeGift)

Angel Marie brightens audiences with her Shine On! message. Her passion and compassion for others is evident in her Shine On! book. Every person, young and old, can always use a spark to ignite or reignite their spirit. Angel Marie, you are Miss Shine On!
—Tanya Brown, Sister of the Late Nicole Brown Simpson

Angel Marie's Shine On! message is an amazing way to learn how to be your original self as well as how to work well with others.
—Mali Creek, 16-year-old High School Student

This message reconnects us with the positivity of honoring one another while respecting ourselves. The Shine On! message also inspires me to think about ideas in a new light. It opens my mind.
—Monique Huerta, 22-year-old Student

The Shine On! message offers delightful, fresh ideas that are inspiring and useful!
—Terri Hardin Jackson, Walt Disney Imagineering

Angel Marie was amazing! She energized the crowd and helped the kids to realize how important it is to be able to read. She brings light to kids' eyes. When she talks about life and love, your heart and mind Shine On! She is a great speaker. I have never found anyone so easy and fun to work with.
—Darin Fishburn, CEO, Reading for Freedom

Angel's name aligns with her message. She truly "Shines" through her words and provides you with the ability to believe you can Shine too!
—Coach Sherry Winn, Two-time Olympian

The Shine On! message has brilliant tips to help anyone discover new ways to listen and take action with wellness.
—Mike Fritz, National College Speaker of the Year Finalist, Founder of Magnetic Speaker, and Founder of Algorithaus for Success

It was such a joy to work with Angel Marie for our event. It's hard for kids to sit still for 20 minutes; they did because Angel Marie was so engaging. We loved the Shine On! message! It really hit home.
—Jaclyn Clark, Event Coordinator, Reading for Freedom

This book is the secret weapon that every person and organization can use to achieve the success they are looking for. Angel Marie Monachelli has put together a collection of unforgettable personal success tips and lifelong strategies in an easy playbook format that are incredibly noteworthy and valuable to all of us. Her 52 secrets are truly magical! Well done!
—John Formica, the Ex-Disney Guy,
America's Customer Experience Speaker and Coach

The Shine On! message inspires and empowers you, your students, and young adults to greater success and happiness.
—Mike Tomasello, CEO of How To Land Any Job.com

A Powerhouse for Transformation and Success

It's amazing how a book can pack so much energy, inspiration, and good, solid direction into a relatively few words. *Shine On!* captures the essence of living well and proposes doable, tiny actions that produce huge positive differences in our experience of life

Each chapter has a theme—like Patience, Abundance, Courage or Trust—that is at the heart of joyful and effective living. Chapters follow a pattern that essentially starts with a paragraph giving the author's definition, a paragraph or two with an engaging anecdote putting flesh and blood on the idea, and a paragraph tying it all into a neat, easy-to-grasp package.

At the end of each chapter is a description of how Shine, the author's Australian Cattle Dog, friend, and muse, demonstrates the concept and an Action Step for making the concept a living part of daily life.

The real power of this book is in the accessibility of the concepts and how easily the Action Steps can be implemented. They are practical and, even more important, they can be fun. That combination sets this book apart from all others offering secrets for personal success, self-esteem, and the ability to help us grow as happy effective individuals, because these are things that readers *will* do. And they produce observable, measurable results almost immediately.

In the end, one of the book's greatest strengths is the compactness of its chapters. While it's suggested to read and practice one chapter a week, this book actually can be consumed in a couple hours. No matter how fast or slow you read it, however, it will change the way you see yourself for the better and produce benefits for the rest of your life.

SHINE ON!

For you Jess,

SHINE ON!

52 SECRETS
For Greater
Success & Higher
Self-esteem

Shine ON!
Angel

ANGEL MARIE MONACHELLI

LIGHTWORKERS PRESS
Phoenix, AZ

Copyright © 2016 Angel Marie Monachelli

LIGHTWORKERS PRESS
Lightworkers Press
24 W. Camelback Rd., Ste. A-413
Phoenix, AZ 85013

Second Edition

All Rights Reserved. No part of this book may be reproduced or transmitted in any form or by any means, electronic or mechanical, including photocopying, recording, or by any informational storage or retrieval system without permission from the publisher.

While all attempts have been made to verify information provided in this book, neither the author nor publisher assumes any responsibility for errors, inaccuracies, or omissions and is not responsible for any financial loss by customer in any manner. Any slights of people or organizations are unintentional.

Printed in the United States of America

Publisher's Cataloging-In-Publication

Names: Monachelli, Angel Marie, author.
Title: Shine on! : 52 secrets for greater success and higher self-esteem / Angel Marie Monachelli.
Description: Second edition. | Phoenix, AZ : Lightworkers Press, [2016]
Identifiers: ISBN: 978-0-9977341-1-9 | 978-0-9977341-8-8 (ebook) | LCCN: 2016916158
Subjects: LCSH: Self-help techniques. | Success. | Success in business. | Self-esteem. | Self-acceptance. | Self-realization. | Self-actualization (Psychology) | Attitude (Psychology) | Quality of life. | BISAC: SELF-HELP / General.
Classification: LCC: BF637.S8 M662 2016 | DDC: 158.1--dc23

Paperback: 978-0-9977341-1-9
eBook: 978-0-9977341-8-8

Book Shepherd: Ellen Reid
Front Cover Design: Lewis Agrell
Interior Design and Layout: Ghislain Viau

*To each of you that have ever been put down,
called stupid, or have felt unloved because of your differences,
know that you can claim success, connect with your personal
power, and Shine On! with higher self-esteem.*

Table of Contents

About the Author ◉ xv
I Wrote This Book for You! ◉ 1
Shine On! Message ◉ 3
Shine's Story ◉ 5

The Secrets

Perception ◉ 7
Enthusiasm ◉ 11
Motivation ◉ 15
Boundaries ◉ 19
Balance ◉ 23
Love ◉ 27
Attitude ◉ 31
Forgiveness ◉ 35
Personal Power ◉ 39
Meditation ◉ 43
Acceptance ◉ 47
Laughter ◉ 51
Awareness ◉ 55
Lack ◉ 59
Exercise ◉ 63

Grief ◉ 67
Success ◉ 71
Communication ◉ 75
Patience ◉ 79
Intuition ◉ 83
Inspiration ◉ 87
Allowing ◉ 91
Happiness ◉ 95
Courage ◉ 99
Wellness ◉ 103
Self-Esteem ◉ 107
Integrity ◉ 111
Spirituality ◉ 115
Honesty ◉ 119
Manifesting ◉ 123

Passion/Purpose ● 127
Shame/Embarrassment ● 131
Appreciation/Gratitude ● 135
Nutrition ● 139
Mission/Goals ● 143
Confidence ● 147
Listening ● 151
Fear ● 155
Play ● 159
Adversity ● 163
Self-Talk ● 167

Abundance ● 171
Aha Moment ● 175
Trust ● 179
Judgment ● 183
Imagination/Creativity ● 187
Honoring/Respect ● 191
Clarity/Peace ● 195
Joy ● 199
Change/Transformation ● 203
Authenticity ● 207
Diversity ● 211

Bonus Freedom ● 215

A Personal Thank You! ● 219

Acknowledgements ● 221

Special FREE Gift for You ● 223

The Ideal Professional Speaker
for Your Next Conference or Event! ● 224

About the Author

Angel Marie Monachelli, founder of the *Shine On!* movement, is a powerhouse in a small package. Diagnosed with dyslexia at an early age, she was called stupid and told she would probably not graduate high school. Though severely challenged she not only graduated, but went on to college on a sports scholarship, receiving her degree, and ultimately becoming one of the youngest players in Women's Major League Softball.

Turning her hard-gained experience overcoming adversity and obstacles into an asset, Angel Marie now travels the country presenting keynote speeches, seminars, workshops, and retreats on effective living and enhancing self-esteem. She is well-known for her energetic presence and engaging exercises that leave audiences of all ages, ethnic backgrounds, and orientations feeling empowered to handle challenges with greater joy and authenticity.

Angel Marie lives in Phoenix, Arizona, with Shine, her awesome Australian Cattle Dog. Through her writing, consulting and workshops she is helping countless people to get their Shine On!

I Wrote This Book for You!

Due to my dyslexia, writing this book was one of my greatest life challenges, yet I knew the Shine On! message would help so many people. By creating *Shine On!*, I have proven to myself that anything is possible, and I am sharing that victory with you to inspire you to overcome the challenges in your life as well.

Shine On! will guide you to increase self-esteem and expand your energy, so that you can achieve success, smile more, and create a great life.

In this guidebook for higher self-confidence and personal success, you will find fifty-two chapters and in each, a simple-to-implement action step. I invite you to complete one action step per week in the span of one year. Using this book, I challenge you to create new habits and develop skills to bring more abundance, freedom, and play into your life.

It is my intention that these pages guide you to express yourself authentically, claim your success, experience the freedom of diversity, and Shine On! I share simple action steps to guide you to discover greater success and achieve higher self-esteem. You will learn about diversity and the importance of respecting differences in others, and how mutual respect helps us succeed in life and create self-confidence. *Shine On!* is especially for anyone seeking to triumph in personal and career goals.

Many of us feel we don't fit in because of ethnicity, personal appearance, or disability. There are millions of reasons why you might feel different than your peers. What matters is discovering that you matter! *Shine On!* shows you how to connect to your authentic self and Shine On!

My canine companion, Shine, has taught me many life lessons about unconditional love and being in the moment. Discover her stories and unique perspective in each chapter.

Shine On!

Shine On! Message

Each one of us has the ability to light up a room! The Shine On! Message is about plugging in to the unique glow inside every one of us!

My dad was an electrician, and I recall a time when I was young and curious about his work. I had no idea that in one moment I would learn about more than just electricity. Looking through his toolbox, my dad pulled out an ampere meter. He asked me to take hold of each of the wired pegs and watch the meter. I was amazed to see the needle jumping about! In that moment, I realized we are all energy.

Shine On! is when we tap into that positive energy and feel the enthusiasm for life and all we do! This light comes from within and allows us to feel joy and freedom! When we feel that Shine On! energy, our bodies respond physically and chemically. Endorphins are released, we have a more adaptive mindset, and we are less likely to become ill. We transform and feel better!

When I am speaking, I ask everyone to stand up and say out loud, "Shine On! Shine On! Shine On!" It energizes us, makes us smile, and brings us joy. It is contagious! Shine On! is about play!

Imagine for a moment if everyone embraced their authentic self and let that beauty Shine On! from the inside out! When we truly love ourselves, we are able to freely accept and appreciate the diversity of others. We are open to seek success and to support others in their goals and missions without fear or judgment.

For example, a fourteen-year-old student at a speaking event shared that the Shine On! message was about smiling more, laughing more, and expressing his own unique style. I couldn't have said it better myself!

I am committed to this mission to guide you to glow with Shine On! energy. I invite you to become a beacon for positive people, brilliant ideas, and amazing success. Be my partner in this movement as we all learn to Shine On! together!

Within these pages are the secrets for personal success, self-esteem, and how the ability to Shine On! can help us all grow as individuals.

Monique Huerta, a twenty-two-year-old student, offers this insightful testimonial: "This message reconnects us with the positivity of honoring one another while respecting ourselves. The Shine On! message also inspires me to think about ideas in a new light. It opens my mind."

Shine's Story

The first time I saw Shine, I felt a deep calm and inner peace. Lisa Maldonado, my best friend and dog trainer, was volunteering at a shelter where thirty dogs had just been rescued from a desperate situation. My beloved Dax had crossed over the Rainbow Bridge two years prior, and I was ready for a new companion. However, I had no idea when Lisa first mentioned an Australian Cattle Dog female to me that it would be love at first sight.

When I walked through the many aisles of the shelter, I didn't see any Australian Cattle Dog.

Then the staff brought out "Hidalgo."

She was beautiful. The sun hit her fur in such a way that Lisa said, "Look, she is glowing with light all around her. Her markings are called 'ticking,' which are also known as 'angel kisses.'" I was in awe!

In the yard, as I watched her play and run, I experienced a feeling of freedom and inner joy, yet I was still speechless and numb.

All of a sudden, I called to her by the name "Shine," and to my surprise she bounded over, plopped down on top of me, and showered me with kisses. At that moment, I felt the connection between Shine and me, and my whole world shifted.

Back at my two-story condo, I laughed as Shine stumbled up and down the unfamiliar stairs. After dinner, I forgot to put some food away, only to discover one Australian Cattle Dog happily chowing down my leftovers on top of the counter. So, stairs might have been an issue, yet heights were definitely not!

Shine quickly began the journey of service-dog training with my friend, Lisa. Shine's loyalty, unconditional love, and willingness to please continue to be amazing gifts. She never judges, and her smile and cuddles bring great joy to all who meet her.

I invite you to read Shine's stories within these pages and let her "messages" speak to you so that you can *Shine On!* with Shine and me.

Shine On!

Secret #1

PERCEPTION

"Maintain a positive perception about yourself, and you will have limitless possibilities in your life."
— Angel Marie

Perception

Either intuitively or through awareness of the world, perception creates your reality. Good perception can help you take positive actions. Perception can inspire us to do amazing things. However, perception can be limiting as well. Attaching emotions to perceptions creates judgments about people, places, or activities. My *Angelisms* are based on my perceptions and experiences with Shine. Your perceptions are based on who you are and your life. Shifting perceptions helps you find success in all you do.

After a speaking event, a woman shared that she wanted to find motivation to lose weight. This woman was close to a healthy size, yet her perception was that she was overweight. After a coaching session, she discovered that her idea of beauty was based on her mother's struggle with obesity. Her mother had projected this onto her daughter throughout her childhood, leading her to believe she, too, was overweight. When she shifted her perception, she was able to find more joy and success in life.

Because I was diagnosed with a learning disability as a child, I struggled with reading and writing in school, yet I never gave up. Teachers and others said I would never amount to anything. If I had listened to their perceptions, I would not have created this book to share with so many about how I was able to overcome these opinions to become the successful person I am today.

SPEAK, SHINE, SPEAK: Shine's perception of her world is in the moment, because she trusts me and feels safe in our routines. She knows her needs are met.

ACTION STEP: Breathe... Write down a perception you have about a situation or person. Define where this view came from. Step out of your comfort zone and redefine this perception in three different ways. And Breathe...

Today I am going to play with perception in this way!

Share your play on Twitter, Facebook, Instagram, Google+
Use #shineonbook

Secret #2

ENTHUSIASM

"Enthusiasm is excitement that inspires, motivates, and creates action."
— Angel Marie

Enthusiasm

Enthusiasm is feeling an energetic interest in a particular subject or activity. It is that spark of light, excitement, and inspiration that spurs us into action. The ability to be excited about opportunities, for no apparent reason, comes from enthusiasm. Enthusiasm is a joyful desire to participate with others. It is choosing to raise your energy level and be excited, even when doing routine activities at home or at work, or things you may not really enjoy, like homework. With more enthusiasm comes greater personal power.

I share my enthusiasm at speaking events with hundreds of people, yet I can be just as enthusiastic when doing mundane tasks. With daily projects, there is a beginning, middle, and end. I choose to look at a responsibility and get excited about the end result.

To create a fun environment, I practice dance movements while sorting clothes, putting them into the washer and dryer, and folding. I say out loud how excited I am about having clean clothes that I like and feel comfortable in. I choose to have fun, even when doing laundry!

SPEAK, SHINE, SPEAK: Shine jumps up and gets enthusiastic when the timer on my phone goes off. She has learned that when my alarm rings, I will be shifting from one activity to another. During this shift, I always create time to pet her, play ball, or give her a treat.

ACTION STEP: Breathe... Train yourself to be enthusiastic. Choose one routine task and play while you do it. Act and feel enthusiastic about it. Sing or play music to get started, and use a timer. When the timer goes off, jump up and get excited to complete the task. Clap. Jump around. Celebrate when you are complete! And Breathe...

Today, I am going to play with enthusiasm in this way!

Share your play on Twitter, Facebook, Instagram, Google+
Use #shineonbook

Secret #3

MOTIVATION

*"Motivation is the spark
that pushes you to change your life."*
— Angel Marie

Motivation

External motivation can come from your parents, a desire for wellness, or from challenges you face in your life. Relying on external motivators, such as a parent telling you what to do, may work better for some people than others.

Internal motivation comes from a gut feeling of wanting to succeed. Internal motivation gives you a push from within that is life-changing. This form of motivation can be learned and practiced. When you have internal motivation, you feel like nothing can stop you. By focusing on the joy of the end result, you can find that feeling of being fired up that gets you to Shine On! and complete any task.

Within two weeks of my first year at the University of Oklahoma, I was flunking every class. Coaches brought me in for a conversation about my grades. I was at risk of being kicked off the softball team and potentially losing my scholarship. Up until this point, I had not told anyone about my learning disability. After learning about my dyslexia, the coaches immediately made a tutor available to me. My motivation was more than the external push from the tutor. I really wanted to play softball and succeed in school. I felt wonderful when I received my Bachelor of Arts in Recreation after focusing and taking on that challenge.

SPEAK, SHINE, SPEAK: Shine performs many helpful tasks. Her motivation is in receiving praise, play, and attention. Shine understands she has done something positive when I give her love or treats, and tell her she is a good girl. This motivates her to continue her positive behavior.

ACTION STEP: Breathe... Create a list of three tasks to complete per day. Assign a small reward that will motivate you to complete each task. And Breathe...

Today I am going to play with motivation in this way!

Share your play on Twitter, Facebook, Instagram, Google+
Use #shineonbook

Secret #4

BOUNDARIES

"Empowering yourself to create healthy boundaries is the framework for a magnificent life."
— Angel Marie

Boundaries

Boundaries are guidelines, rules, or limits created by you. These limits identify reasonable, permissible ways for others to behave around you. Boundaries dictate how you respond when someone crosses your limits. Creating positive boundaries is focusing on positive outcomes. Boundaries are a mix of beliefs and experiences, which are different for everyone. You are entitled to your boundaries! Healthy boundaries create self-worth and connect you with greater success in life.

After a speaking event, a woman shared her example of boundaries. At work, if anyone complains about personal relationships, she politely and with love tells them she is not comfortable talking about personal business. She puts an end to the conversation before she is drawn into it. This is brilliant, because this boundary creates a safe work environment.

When I am in a group, one-on-one, or on social media, I have boundaries about politics, religion, and horror movies (because they give me the creeps). These are topics I choose not to engage in. In conversation, I politely excuse myself. On social media, I scroll past and do not respond.

I also practice boundaries when using my cell phone: I choose to be the master of this handy device rather than a slave to it! My phone is on silent mode most of the time, and I choose to keep it in my purse at restaurants. By keeping my cell phone in the other room when I go to bed, I am creating a boundary so that I can sleep in peace.

SPEAK, SHINE, SPEAK: Shine has rules for everything. Shine's rules help her routinely understand her boundaries. By creating structure such as when to eat, get her toys, and go for walks, Shine is more relaxed and listens better.

ACTION STEP: Breathe... When sitting down to eat, silence your phone and remove it from the table, or leave it in another room. And Breathe...

Today I am going to play with boundaries in this way!

Share your play on Twitter, Facebook, Instagram, Google+
Use #shineonbook

Secret #5

BALANCE

"The secret to balance is inner peace expressed through joyful movement."
— Angel Marie

Balance

Balance is more than juggling the external demands of personal time, work, and school. Balance is also about finding clarity, feeling calm, and being grounded. Feeling unbalanced comes when you allow yourself to be pulled by external forces and situations that are not in alignment with your own needs. Taking time to do things you enjoy will help you to focus and to feel even more joy.

Balance is a feeling of confidence that everything is going to work out just fine. Internal and external balance increases personal power and awareness, because it guides us to seek out harmonious environments and sense when others are in chaos.

Balance for me is about creating a physical space where I feel comfortable to work and play. I am balanced internally and externally when my office is clean and decorated with things that bring me joy. An environment in disarray makes my mind feel as scattered as the papers on the desk. All it takes for me to create internal balance is to throw out, clean up, and declutter my living and work space. Once my desk is clean, I experience clarity, and I am able to be more productive and feel more successful.

SPEAK, SHINE, SPEAK: I know Shine is balanced when she is able to relax and lie at my feet peacefully. When Shine is not listening and cannot be still, she is clearly out of balance. Shine's trainer, Lisa, says that the dogs she works with are often out of balance. She guides owners to provide physical and mental outlets to create a balanced environment for their dogs.

ACTION STEP: Breathe... Pick one project today. Before starting, create an organized and clean workspace. When the task is complete, put everything away. And Breathe...

Today I am going to play with balance in this way!

Share your play on Twitter, Facebook, Instagram, Google+
Use #shineonbook

Secret #6

LOVE

*"The shine of a smile is
a simple act of shared love."*
— Angel Marie

Love

Everyone looks at and experiences love differently. The ability to be loved and feel love starts with self-love. Creating boundaries within relationships is an act of self-love. Loving a person for every version of themselves connects us on a deeper level. Unconditional love is accepting people or ideas without judgment. Accepting the love of others, and ourselves, is an act of embracing our self-worth.

Allowing your partner to spend free time with family or friends without constantly texting him or her is a positive relationship boundary.

At a camp retreat, one of the campers wanted to experience more love. We discussed how she could share unconditional love by giving without expecting anything in return. She chose to make friendship bracelets and hide them in the campers' shoes while they were swimming. It was wonderful to watch her energy shift as she expressed love in her own way and experienced the joyful reactions of the other campers.

What I recognized about my dad's love was that he accepted his children for who they were in each stage of life. My stepmother shared with me that after my dad and I would have our Monday lunch dates, he would come home to her and ask, "How do I get Angel to see that she does not have to do anything, or be anything, for me to love her?" It was at this point that I understood what unconditional love is: accepting and loving a person for who they are. Always.

SPEAK, SHINE, SPEAK: Dogs, in general, offer loyalty and unconditional love. Shine offers love by always wanting to please me and by giving awesome kisses.

ACTION STEP: Breathe... Every time you look in the mirror, say, "I love you." Use your first and middle name. Repeat three times. And Breathe...

Today I am going to play with love in this way!

_____
_____
_____
_____
_____
_____
_____
_____

Share your play on Twitter, Facebook, Instagram, Google+
Use #shineonbook

Secret #7

ATTITUDE

"Shift your attitude and gain greater freedom."
— Angel Marie

Attitude

Attitude is a small part of life that makes a huge difference. Attitude is the predisposition to respond positively or negatively towards ideas, people, or situations. How you feel about a situation or person is created by your attitude. Choosing a new attitude creates a new life.

I did not think much about my natural ability as an athlete until high school. I developed a positive outlook about sports and my skills. Even changing schools due to my parents' divorce, I always knew I had a place on the field. This propelled me forward in sports. I was the youngest to play on a major league women's softball team while I was still in high school. By the time I started at Golden West Junior College, I had a real hot-dog attitude.

This was not the case in my classes. In high school, I asked a teacher to spell a word for me. In response, he yelled at me to get a dictionary and look it up myself. I couldn't even start spelling the first letters of the word to be able to look it up. I felt embarrassed and stupid. This incident, and others, created an attitude of anger that built up inside of me about reading and writing. I grew to resent comments about my writing skills. This had a serious impact on my growth and learning. It was difficult for me to ask for help until a tutor shifted my attitude.

SPEAK, SHINE, SPEAK: Shine's attitude is always loving and joyful. Her trainer, Lisa, says dogs mirror the energy of their owners.

ACTION STEP: Breathe... Before leaving your house, look in the mirror, smile, and say out loud, "I feel awesome today!" And Breathe...

Today I am going to play with attitude in this way!

_____
_____
_____
_____
_____
_____
_____
_____
_____

Share your play on Twitter, Facebook, Instagram, Google+
Use #shineonbook

Secret #8

FORGIVENESS

*"True forgiveness gives freedom
to every heart involved."*
— Angel Marie

Forgiveness

Forgiveness is choosing to accept the way you understand reality. In some cases, forgiveness is letting go of relationships, situations, or personal perceptions that no longer serve you. Letting go of emotional connections can be challenging, yet to learn to let go of an emotional connection that is not in your best interest is a key part of embracing your self-worth. As you release anger and resentment, you experience room for success in everything you do.

After a speaking event, a young woman told me she felt resentment towards herself because of her past life choices. She acknowledged that it was time for her to start over and forgive herself. By rebuilding positive relationships, such as spending time with close friends and family instead of passing acquaintances at bars and clubs, she allowed herself to recognize her true value, improve self-esteem, and find happiness.

One of my best friends decided she no longer wanted to continue our relationship. I felt I must have done something wrong as a friend. I was hurt, yet I worked through the emotions and realized her choice had nothing to do with me. Forgiveness came when I stopped taking her choice personally and stepped into realizing that whatever she was experiencing was based on her perception of our relationship.

SPEAK, SHINE, SPEAK: Because Shine was abused before she came to me, I believe her process of forgiveness was to learn to trust again. It took time and patience to get her to relax and feel safe around me and other people.

ACTION STEP: Breathe... Pick one personal situation that you are having trouble releasing. Write it down on a piece of paper. Rip it up and throw it away. Let yourself cry and release the energy and emotions of that experience. And Breathe...

Today I am going to play with forgiveness in this way!

Share your play on Twitter, Facebook, Instagram, Google+
Use #shineonbook

Secret #9

PERSONAL POWER

*"Personal power is accepting
and acting upon your uniqueness."*
— Angel Marie

Personal Power

We are born with our own unique personal power. With personal power, we make better choices, experience more positive relationships, attain the ability to bounce back from adversity, and create empowering opportunities. Some people give away their personal power by believing they are victims, or that the opinions of others have control over their choices. Having personal power brings joy, passion, and growth. The greater you feel your personal power, the more limitless success you will experience.

In grammar school, I was challenged by reading and writing. I feared the opinions of others, so I didn't talk about it. When I finally found the strength to ask for help, I discovered that the tutors didn't judge me or my dyslexia and were wonderful guides to my success. I gained greater personal power by asking for help and guidance in creating ways of learning that worked best for me.

A coaching client shared how her eyes were opened to conducting herself with higher integrity after our session. A teacher had given her an A on an essay, yet a friend recognized spelling and grammar errors. She could have blown it off. However, she chose to be in her personal power, fix the essay, and take a closer look at future assignments. A year later, she connected with me to announce that she graduated *summa cum laude*.

SPEAK, SHINE, SPEAK: Shine was mistreated as a puppy. She regained her personal power when she was able to trust people and accept me as her new companion. Shine's personal power is limitless because of her innate ability to love unconditionally, forgive, and live in the moment.

ACTION STEP: Breathe... Write down five things you are proud to tell others you are successful at. Post this list in a visible location. Repeat daily. And Breathe...

Today I am going to play with personal power in this way!

Share your play on Twitter, Facebook, Instagram, Google+
Use #shineonbook

Secret #10

MEDITATION

*"Meditation is a practice to achieve peace
and harmony in your life."*
— Angel Marie

Meditation

Meditation is the ability to concentrate on one thing while letting all other thoughts flow away. There are many forms of meditation, including prayer, music, silence, candles, lying down, or sitting up. Meditation can even be done while you are performing mundane tasks. Meditation can reduce stress, foster good physical health, and increase happiness. Meditation is a practice that can be improved upon over time. Surrounded as we all are by invasive technology and ever-evolving forms of communication, meditation allows you to stop and listen to the voice within you. It is a way to raise self-esteem, be more productive, and create greater success on all levels.

As a junior at the University of Oklahoma, I experienced challenges with my back. The coaches contacted a relaxation specialist to teach me the art of breathing. This training opened me up to the realization that I was a backwards breather. I was taught the correct way to breathe, which is to inhale, diaphragm out, and then exhale, diaphragm in. To this day, I use this breathing method to achieve relaxation and focus.

A young client shared with me that exams gave him anxiety. We created a three-step routine to perform before each test. He took time to count breaths on the walk to the classroom. When seated, he adjusted his posture, starting at his shoulders and ending with his feet on the floor. He finished this process by spending a moment to envision passing the test, and taking a deep breath before picking up his pencil. Using these steps, he was able to calm himself and be more productive and successful in school and life.

SPEAK, SHINE, SPEAK: Shine meditates daily to help her ground, relax, and process.

ACTION STEP: Breathe... Be still and silent at the same time. Focus and breathe rhythmically. Start out with two minutes and increase daily to twenty minutes. And Breathe...

Today I am going to play with meditation in this way!

Share your play on Twitter, Facebook, Instagram, Google+
Use #shineonbook

Secret #11

ACCEPTANCE

*"Acceptance generates a connection
to your awesome inner Shine."*
— Angel Marie

Acceptance

Acceptance happens by embracing your authenticity and respecting the views or actions of others. Acceptance is understanding that everything has a purpose, even if you don't know what that purpose is. While acceptance from others is important, true acceptance comes from within. A lack of acceptance is often displayed by argumentative behavior or an attitude of negativity. A lack of acceptance of yourself or others can negatively impact your wellness. You empower yourself when you accept a situation that you do not agree with; you can agree to disagree.

One of my best friends was diagnosed with terminal cancer. He continued to eat whatever he wanted. He denied chemo. I struggled with his decisions. When I finally accepted he wasn't being hardheaded, and that it was his choice, I felt unconditional love for him. He lived in his own way, and spent his last days on his own terms. He was always his authentic self.

When I think of acceptance, I envision my dad's license plate on his car. My dad had a saying: "I okay, you okay." As long as we each accept who we are, as well as give space for others to be who they are, we will all be okay. This was so much a part of who he was that he had a special plate made: IOK-UOK. Many people would smile and say what a great message he was sharing. I am honored to display his plate on my car and continue sharing this message.

SPEAK, SHINE, SPEAK: Shine is in total acceptance of herself. She never wishes she was a Pekingese or another breed.

ACTION STEP: Breathe... Write down five things you accept about yourself, and five things you can be more accepting of in others. Do this every night before you go to bed. And Breathe...

Today I am going to play with acceptance in this way!

Share your play on Twitter, Facebook, Instagram, Google+
Use #shineonbook

Secret #12

LAUGHTER

"I love to laugh. Even a fake laugh can make your body feel good. Try it!"
— Angel Marie

Laughter

Laughter is contagious. It creates joy and just feels good! When we laugh together, we learn together, and it unites us. Laughter helps build self-esteem and self-worth, and it helps you shift your perception. Sometimes, we can be too serious and forget to laugh. We are drawn to groups who are laughing and having a good time. When we can laugh at ourselves, we can see that our setbacks are only temporary.

A seventeen-year-old client of mine wanted to laugh. This was a challenge because he didn't think anything was funny. I shared some action steps with him so that he could practice laughing, including fake laughter. A fake laugh has the same energy as real laughter. Over time, he felt more relaxed, happier, and could feel his self-esteem rising. He learned how to laugh for real.

When I am a vendor at a conference, one of my favorite things to do is create laughter with everyone. Sometimes, we start with a funny nonsense word like "Hoowah!" Once a few people start laughing, others are drawn in to find out what the ruckus is about. Suddenly, all eyes are on us, wondering what is so funny. I love bringing people together in this way!

SPEAK, SHINE, SPEAK: Even Shine laughs! When she is excited or having a lot of fun, she howls. She cannot hold in all that joy. It bubbles out in a nice long howl of laughter. I even have a video on my website of her howling, because that makes me laugh.

ACTION STEP: Breathe... Take time every morning to look in the mirror and make yourself laugh at least three times. Start with a giggle and work up to a full belly laugh! And Breathe...

Today I am going to play with laughter in this way!

_____
_____
_____
_____
_____
_____
_____
_____
_____

Share your play on Twitter, Facebook, Instagram, Google+
Use #shineonbook

Secret #13

AWARENESS

"Awareness is the electrifying moment that ignites your action."
— Angel Marie

Awareness

Awareness is a multifaceted skill that requires practice and patience. It comes from listening to intuition, understanding signals from the environment, and analyzing experiences. When in an unsafe situation, or following a poor choice, using awareness can guide you to sanctuary. Awareness is the ability to experience situations, interpret actions, and analyze emotions with an open mind.

The current generation will graduate from high school with access to more information from Google, YouTube, and social media than the previous generation encountered by the end of college. With this knowledge comes a requirement for discernment. When reading or sharing a post on social media, taking the time to research the source can be critical to your integrity.

A caller on a radio program complained that her kids were unmotivated and disrespectful, and she felt unappreciated. By using tough love, she took back her personal power and held her kids accountable for their actions. Using stipulations and rewards, her family became aware of how to create a harmonious home.

My most beautiful moment of awareness lasted only a second, yet I will never forget it. I was in high school and came home shocked to find my room completely cleared out for a surprise move to an apartment. This sudden reality of my parents' divorce shook me to the core. I realized this move would also mean it was time to take on more responsibility instead of simply being the baby of the family.

SPEAK, SHINE, SPEAK: Shine is an Australian Cattle Dog, which is a herding breed. She is highly aware of her surroundings. She scans as she walks down the street, fully and totally aware.

ACTION STEP: Breathe... Mentally put yourself back into a situation or conflict from the day. Write down actions, emotions, dialogue, and body language that you recall. Write down any actions you would change. And Breathe...

Today I am going to play with awareness in this way!

Share your play on Twitter, Facebook, Instagram, Google+
Use #shineonbook

Secret #14

LACK

"Lack is an illusion. There are always more crayons to create your world!"
— Angel Marie

Lack

Lack is an illusion that stems from a place of fear—thinking we do not have enough. To feel lack is to indicate the absence of something desirable, important, or necessary to our lives. Lack can have an impact on your life, even when you may not realize it. Stress is related to lack in that it creates a sense of urgency in our own minds.

Nature does not have a lack mentality. I live in Phoenix, which is a desert environment that lacks water. The cactus, however, has adapted to thrive without concern for that lack.

When I was at Golden West Junior College, I had a scholarship that only covered my housing; food and other essentials weren't included. My three roommates were in the same situation. A noticeable lack mentality existed among us. Instead of sharing, we would watch each other suspiciously and sometimes even hide food. I felt stressed and unfocused at times because of the perception of lack of food, even though I never went hungry and could ask for help from friends and family at any time.

When I was growing up, my dad would say, "Money doesn't grow on trees." I carried that mentality of not enough money into my adult life until I found my passion. By working hard and focusing on my coaching business, I created success in a career I love. There are no limits when we love what we do.

SPEAK, SHINE, SPEAK: Shine doesn't have a lack mentality because she lives in the moment. She doesn't focus on her past when she wasn't given enough food.

ACTION STEP: Breathe... Before you get out of bed, say three times, "I have all that I desire, and I am abundant." And Breathe...

Today I am going to play with recognizing lack in this way!

_____
_____
_____
_____
_____
_____
_____
_____

Share your play on Twitter, Facebook, Instagram, Google+
Use #shineonbook

Secret #15

EXERCISE

"Exercise is personal power in action."

— Angel Marie

Exercise

Exercise is important for keeping the physical body functioning properly and helping the mind to be focused and active. Exercise can reduce stress, elevate your mood, and nurture self-esteem. Without movement, the mind can become dull and tired. Even a few minutes of movement between long sessions of seated work can increase productivity. Social sports, games, and meditative movement such as yoga or Tai Chi are all beneficial forms of exercise.

Dance and movement have always been an important part of my life. My mama operated a dance studio for many years, and from the age of two, I was dancing. In school, I was happier in a Physical Education class than sitting still. Ever since I was a little kid, exercise and play helped me to become more relaxed and focused.

Even now, despite health challenges and the lingering effects of sports injuries and car accidents, I still continue to exercise and play. I love swimming because it allows me to continue exercising my body through nearly weightless movement, and it improves my mental focus. Before walking Shine, I practice stretching and breathing techniques in order to nurture my body safely and gently.

SPEAK, SHINE, SPEAK: Animals need exercise, too! When Shine starts to get hyper, I know it is time to play. Shine releases excess energy by playing and being obsessive about her squeaky ball. For more fun, I hide her ball in the blankets for her to dig out. This is mental and physical exercise for Shine.

ACTION STEP: Breathe... If you are seated for more than an hour, set a timer. When the timer goes off, get up and move for at least ten minutes. This is not the time to get on the phone or check social media. And Breathe...

Today I am going to play with exercise in this way!

Share your play on Twitter, Facebook, Instagram, Google+
Use #shineonbook

Secret #16

GRIEF

*"Grief is the gift we release
to attain greater happiness."*
— Angel Marie

Grief

Grief is sorrow or extreme sadness from loss or worry. Grief comes in many forms—from heartbreak to death. Some grief stems from feeling powerless because of another person's actions or decisions. How you cope with grief is unique to you. Grief has no time limit. Allowing the process of grief, and accepting the emotions connected to it, helps us be successful in our personal and professional lives.

In a group webinar, I spoke with a young man who had lost his job and his dog, and his aunt had passed away. He had guilt because he felt more grief over the death of his dog than anything else. We talked about how grieving for his dog did not lessen his love or emotional connection to his aunt. Only then was he able to allow himself to have crying sessions. Shortly thereafter, he emailed me that he had found success in a new job and the love of a new puppy.

At the celebration of life for my dad, I felt that there were expectations for me to be the source of support and strength that I typically am. Yet I continually separated myself from the group to cry in private. Because I chose to grieve in my own way, I gained greater emotional clarity to heal, and I found a deeper love for myself and my dad.

SPEAK, SHINE, SPEAK: When I leave the house, it is important that I give Shine a job, such as watching the house. When I leave for more than two days, my amazing dog sitters tell me that Shine seems sad. In her mind, I am gone forever, because she thinks like a two-year-old. I believe this is a form of grief.

ACTION STEP: Breathe… Give yourself permission to cry to release your grief. Say out loud, "I release grief and accept happiness in my life." And Breathe…

Today I am going to play with giving myself permission to grieve in this way!

Share your play on Twitter, Facebook, Instagram, Google+
Use #shineonbook

Secret #17

SUCCESS

*"When we like who we are, what we do,
and where we are, true success is guaranteed."*
— Angel Marie

Success

Everyone perceives success differently. Society often measures success by one's income, fame, or status. Recognition—such as trophies, ribbons, or certificates for achievements or goals met—is a celebration of success.

Our personal values and passions can be a wonderful way to define what success means to each of us. When you are happy with what you do, you feel successful. Your success is limitless! Personal success brings greater self-esteem. Celebrate your successes, big or small, every day.

Graduating from the University of Oklahoma was an awesome personal success for me. It took courage for me to ask for help and stay inspired. I celebrated small successes after tests, completion of major projects, and at the end of every semester. Wonderful tutors and coaches guided me along the way to receive my Bachelor of Arts in Recreation. I may have invested five years in college to complete a four-year degree, yet I did it!

SPEAK, SHINE, SPEAK: Shine understands success, too. She is an Australian Cattle Dog, which is a working breed. Shine's trainer, Lisa, told me this breed is accustomed to working hard and having things to do. It is important that Shine has tasks to do in her domestic life so she can feel successful. To Shine, when I tell her to watch the house while I am out, or to bring my sneakers, she is doing an important job. As Shine's alpha companion, it is up to me to let her know she is successful by telling her she is a good girl.

ACTION STEP: Breathe... Write your list of tasks for the day. As you complete them, write "Shine On!" to celebrate. And Breathe...

Today I am going to play with success in this way!

Share your play on Twitter, Facebook, Instagram, Google+
Use #shineonbook

Secret #18

COMMUNICATION

*"Create clarity in all your communications
and you will Shine On!"*
— Angel Marie

Communication

Communication is an exchange of information between others and yourself. Communication involves speaking, seeing, touching, and listening for a deeper one-on-one connection. Computers and mobile devices have both expanded and limited communication. We communicate with people on the other side of the world, yet do we understand their feelings? In most cases, sadly, no. When you look at the person you are talking to, a positive emotional connection is created that can make both people feel valued and appreciated.

A radio show caller expressed the feeling that he was wasting time on social media, clicking away aimlessly. His list of friends was in the thousands, yet he felt disconnected. I shared with him ways to overcome his feeling of disconnection. Of the ideas discussed, he chose to set a timer as an indicator to walk away from the computer, replace social media time with another activity, and have someone else hold his account password. I asked him to call me to talk him through the first week or so. After a few weeks, he had created a social media schedule that allowed him more time to meet friends face to face.

When I meet someone, I hug them, smile, and make eye contact. During conversation, I tend to make physical contact by touching their arm or shoulder. I start and end conversations with a smile. These gestures are important aspects of communication that my friends on social media miss.

SPEAK, SHINE, SPEAK: When Shine wants me to get moving, she uses nonverbal cues such as nudging me with her nose. She also howls when she is really excited. These are some of the ways Shine communicates.

ACTION STEP: Breathe... Once a day, have an in-person, face-to-face conversation. Be attentive to gestures, eye contact, and facial expressions. And Breathe...

Today I am going to play with communication in this way!

Share your play on Twitter, Facebook, Instagram, Google+
Use #shinconbook

Secret #19

PATIENCE

*"Patience is an active, purposeful,
and wonderful form of personal power."*
— Angel Marie

Patience

Patience is the ability to remain calm when dealing with difficulties, annoying situations, or stressful people. Patience is a valuable character trait that is learned and must be practiced. The act of being patient appears passive, yet patience is an active, purposeful, and wonderful form of self-discipline. Having patience helps you to achieve greater clarity.

I have always been a multitasker, maybe because I get so enthusiastic about life. I confess I do feel scattered at times. Focusing on patience while I wait in line—rather than on what I want to have happen in the future—helps me feel more balanced. Simply concentrating on gratitude for what I am experiencing in the moment allows me to feel less frustrated and more even-tempered when circumstances are out of my control.

Another way I practice patience is by sitting at my kitchen table to eat. After each bite of food, I set my utensil down, place my hands in my lap, and wait a few seconds after swallowing before taking another mouthful.

SPEAK, SHINE, SPEAK: When I first brought Shine home, she ate so fast. This was probably because she was in shelters for the first eight months of her life and had to fight for her food. To help Shine slow down, I trained her to sit and wait before she eats. Because Shine wants to please me, she practices this self-discipline and is rewarded for it. Through this practice, she learned impulse control, which in "dog speak" is patience.

ACTION STEP: Breathe... Be mindful of how fast you are moving, then s-l-o-w down. When eating, put your utensil down between bites. And Breathe...

Today I am going to play with patience in this way!

Share your play on Twitter, Facebook, Instagram, Google+
Use #shineonbook

Secret #20

INTUITION

"Daydreaming is the gift of an intuitive mind."

— Angel Marie

Intuition

Intuition is a gut feeling you experience when shifting from one situation to another. Your intuition can guide you out of unsafe environments or create amazing situations. Paying attention to that first reaction, or the little voice in your head, is a valuable part of intuition. You might get a sense to take a different route when walking home from school, and then find a twenty-dollar bill on the ground. Your intuition led you there. Intuition can also be the act of going against the norm and trusting your inner self even when no one else does. Some people may think you are weird or uncool, yet it always pays to follow your intuition.

In high school, I was invited to a party. I felt uncomfortable when I arrived. The party was crowded, and everyone was having fun, yet I still felt something was not right. After a short time, I told my friends that I was leaving. They were disappointed, yet they joined me. The next day, we found out the party had gotten out of hand. Many students were arrested. This event helped me realize how important it is to listen to my intuition. As I grew, I learned to never second-guess my intuition.

SPEAK, SHINE, SPEAK: Animals always pay attention to their intuition. Shine knows when someone needs love, and shows this by sitting on their feet. Shine's trainer, Lisa, says this is instinctive. Shine is also a great judge of character. She will let me know how she feels about people we meet. If you have pets, you may have noticed how they react before a storm or earthquake. Animals trust their intuition and act accordingly to communicate the message.

ACTION STEP: Breathe... When entering a new situation or meeting a new person, take a breath and connect to your intuition. Pay attention to your first reaction to this person or situation. And Breathe...

Today I am going to play with intuition in this way!

Share your play on Twitter, Facebook, Instagram, Google+
Use #shineonbook

Secret #21

INSPIRATION

*"Inspiration is an inner power
that activates outer change."*
— Angel Marie

Inspiration

Inspiration is the process of being mentally stimulated to do or feel something. It is a brilliant idea that arouses your desire to take action. Inspiration is a deep inner feeling that moves you to be more creative and enthusiastic in life. Inspiration is a feeling that can be learned and practiced. Sometimes a life lesson, unexpected health issue, or relationship change can drive inspiration.

When applied to health and wellness, the desire to feel good can inspire us to exercise or eat healthy food. Over a decade ago, I was diagnosed with lupus, fibromyalgia, and arthritis. I was a size zero, had a persistent cough, and felt severely fatigued. These illnesses inspired me to improve my health. I was driven to change my habits. I hired a nutritionist and learned how certain foods could be beneficial to my health. I experimented with cooking and found joy in the kitchen for the first time.

I have been called "the catalyst," "the motivator," and sometimes "the cheerleader" by my clients and friends. I also go to others for inspiration. On weekends, I lead an Inspiration and Coffee Meetup group in Central Phoenix. We share brilliant, creative, and awesome ideas that inspire all of us. This type of gathering helps everyone stay energized, be more productive, and feel empowered all week long. Finding like-minded people is an amazing way to stay inspired!

SPEAK, SHINE, SPEAK: Food and treats inspire Shine! When I let her know she did a good job and listened to a command, she is inspired to do it again.

ACTION STEP: Breathe... Kick-start your energy after lunch with movement such as running, walking, or dancing. And Breathe...

Today, I am going to play with inspiration in this way!

Share your play on Twitter, Facebook, Instagram, Google+
Use #shineonbook

Secret #22

ALLOWING

"Shining On is allowing your light to glow."
— Angel Marie

Allowing

Allowing is letting things be as they are. It is letting go of questioning or anticipation. It is a feeling of security and knowing. This ability to be in the moment opens the way for total joy. Allowing is releasing expectations of situations and relationships. Growing from personal setbacks and creating positive comebacks is a big part of allowing. Practicing allowing helps you to raise your self-esteem, reduce stress, and achieve greater success.

Social media is a space where we can practice allowing. We can even agree to disagree without comment. A member of a social media group I moderate messaged me about another member's excessive use of quizzes. She felt annoyed and wanted to block this person's posts. We talked about how the art of allowing sometimes means not engaging. She understood she could scroll past that person's posts or hide them and let it go.

At the University of Oklahoma, I had a set schedule for classes and practices. Knowing what to expect next allowed me to feel secure in taking things one day at a time. By embracing this routine, the vision of my graduation felt like a certainty, rather than something to stress over. Allowing my life to unfold helped me feel more personal empowerment.

SPEAK, SHINE, SPEAK: Animals, like Shine, are brilliant at allowing. Shine will roll over, completely exposing her underside. Lying there, stretched out, she will fall asleep. In dog language, this is the most vulnerable position. She is allowing herself to be vulnerable because she feels safe.

ACTION STEP: Breathe... Each day say out loud three times, "I release any people, places, or things that do not serve me. I allow positive experiences to come into my life." And Breathe...

Today, I am going to play with allowing in this way!

Share your play on Twitter, Facebook, Instagram, Google+
Use #shineonbook

Secret #23

HAPPINESS

*"Happiness is feeling like
you are on vacation all the time."*
— Angel Marie

Happiness

Happiness is a choice we make every moment. The practice of happiness creates the energy to be inspired and motivated. Happiness is focusing on the good feeling we have when a job is completed. Happiness helps us build a deeper connection with others and ourselves. Being part of a team or being in a relationship that feels positive brings happiness. Happiness combined with the right action ultimately equal success.

When we play a video game, the activity on the screen is not physically real, yet we feel the joy of getting to the finish line or capturing the prize. That happy feeling comes from within!

After watching my positive and empowering videos on YouTube, a young woman commented that she wanted to look at life with a more optimistic attitude. She focused on the feelings of happiness, and she was able to turn her life around. By seeing the bright side, and smiling as she entered into new experiences, she felt less stressed and more energetic. She was offered better opportunities because people wanted to work alongside her. She even reported she was able to recover from a cold faster!

I am conscious about my level of happiness and how I feel in my life. When I walk Shine in my neighborhood, I choose to practice happiness by waving, smiling, and saying hello. Happiness is contagious! Sharing positive energy that spreads happiness raises everyone's self-esteem.

SPEAK, SHINE, SPEAK: I believe Shine communicates her happiness though her crazy, obsessive kissing. When she greets you, she will bathe you in kisses. Especially your feet!

ACTION STEP: Breathe... Every day in the shower, sing, "I am happy! I share happy! Happy feels great! I love happy!" Say it. Sing it. Write it. And Breathe...

Today I am going to play with happiness in this way!

Share your play on Twitter, Facebook, Instagram, Google+
Use #shinconbook

Secret #24

COURAGE

"Greater courage comes from accepting and acknowledging your vulnerability."
— Angel Marie

Courage

Whether you know it or not, you are courageous! It takes strength and personal power to act when the odds seem stacked against you. Stepping outside of your comfort zone may be perceived as being crazy, yet courage can be as simple as believing "you've got this." It takes courage to embrace your authentic self and act upon it. Practicing courage involves releasing self-doubt, old beliefs, and criticism. When being courageous, look for safety first and trust your intuition.

My BFF Kaya has the courage to pursue a career dominated by men. She works as an inspector on the Alaska pipeline—a field where there are few women. When traveling, Kaya relies on intuition to steer clear of harmful situations. Following an uncomfortable feeling about a particular job site, she had the courage to return to camp and request reassignment. While traveling to her new site, she heard that a blizzard stranded the crew at the previous site. With courage and intuition, Kaya has created a life that gives her freedom and a job she loves.

In the 1980s, I worked toward my Doctorate of Motors. I was the only woman in the automotive department. I felt comfortable. Others said I was crazy. Looking back, it took courage to be a woman in that male-dominated environment. I realized my courage when my car broke down on a desolate road. I opened my toolbox and fixed the problem. Driving away, I felt self-reliant, empowered, and proud that I had effectively utilized my training.

SPEAK, SHINE, SPEAK: Shine is innately courageous because she is a herding breed, an Australian Cattle Dog.

ACTION STEP: Breathe... Repeat several times during the day, "I am courageous because..." and say three things that make you feel courageous. And Breathe...

Today I am going to play with courage in this way!

Share your play on Twitter, Facebook, Instagram, Google+
Use #shineonbook

Secret #25

WELLNESS

"Amazing wellness is created by a healthy mind and proper physical alignment."
— Angel Marie

Wellness

Wellness is about feeling good! We experience wellness on all levels—spiritual, mental, emotional, and physical. Creating positive boundaries is a part of wellness that can reduce stress, increase energy, and promote peace. Practicing wellness with healthy eating and exercise is an expression of self-worth. Listening to your inner voice is an important step toward achieving wellness.

In Phoenix, when I speak to athletes and school sports teams, I emphasize the importance of drinking plenty of water. Staying hydrated is one key to having more energy, being more focused, and feeling more confident. We discuss how drinking enough water is an easy way to look better and feel better.

In my teen years, I was slim and athletic no matter what I ate. After three car accidents, this changed. My inability to exercise and my unhealthy eating habits caused me to gain weight and feel depressed. I felt slow, tired, and low on energy. Seeing wellness in a new light, I educated myself on nutrition and the best fuel to put in my body. By eating a more balanced diet, I felt happier and more energized. I even slept better.

SPEAK, SHINE, SPEAK: I help Shine take care of her wellness by only offering her good foods. Yet I have noticed that when her biscuits get stale, she will not eat them.

ACTION STEP: Breathe... Measure your weight in pounds. Cut that number in half. This number is how many ounces of water some health experts recommend per day. At the end of the day, celebrate your water intake! And Breathe…

Today I am going to play with wellness in this way!

_____
_____
_____
_____
_____
_____
_____
_____

Share your play on Twitter, Facebook, Instagram, Google+
Use #shineonbook

Secret #26

SELF~ESTEEM

"When you Shine with healthy self-esteem, challenges and self-doubt fall away."
— Angel Marie

Self-Esteem

Self-esteem is complete acceptance of yourself and confidence in your abilities. The attitude of positive self-esteem creates limitless possibilities, powerful opportunities, and awesome relationships. With greater self-esteem, every setback is followed by a more powerful comeback. Healthy self-esteem is the armor that shields against challenges and self-doubt. Boosting your self-esteem is a mental practice that can increase your happiness and success in life.

A podcast show caller expressed feeling inadequate compared to others his age. We discussed how a negative, inaccurate view of self can be sabotaging. I invited him to write out his negative self-talk so he could see it. When we spoke again, his whole attitude had changed. He was able to see how harsh his inner voice had been. He realized that speaking to anyone in this way created self-doubt, so he shifted his perceptions. Rather than talking himself out of calculated risks, self-talk connected him to empowering relationships and opportunities. He became his own most enthusiastic and vocal cheerleader!

As a keynote speaker, I share how negative self-esteem is one of the most common issues, especially among women and young people. Studies have shown that many people have diminished self-esteem because of the perceived opinions of others. Their positive light is dulled because they're comparing themselves to the ideals put forth by the media and society. The three tips I offer to raise self-esteem are to smile, breathe, and laugh. I have seen people's lives change due to these powerful yet simple actions.

SPEAK, SHINE, SPEAK: Shine's self-esteem is built on praise, learning new tasks, and having a job to do.

ACTION STEP: Breathe... Every night write down three positive aspects about yourself. And Breathe...

Today I am going to play with self-esteem in this way!

Share your play on Twitter, Facebook, Instagram, Google+
Use #shineonbook

Secret #27

INTEGRITY

"Inspire integrity by choosing honest thoughts and actions."
— Angel Marie

Integrity

Integrity is the act of being honest in behavior, work, and action. Integrity is living your life according to a code of moral principles. It takes courage to live a life of integrity. Sometimes it seems easier to tell a little white lie than speak the truth, yet valuing integrity is doing what is right. Recognizing integrity in yourself helps you see it in others. When expressed with love, speaking with integrity is a powerful way to reveal your authentic self.

In grammar school, the students in the special class were called stupid because of our learning disabilities. I was rarely bullied, though, because I simply wouldn't take it. I defended one of the blind students from a boy who was pushing her. I was so angry I pushed him into a tree! I knew that this was not the proper action, yet I wanted to defend my friend. With integrity, I walked myself to the principal's office, told him what I'd done, and accepted the punishment.

One of my friends was concerned about a teacher who lacked integrity. He shared that the teacher had been intentionally allowing some students to pass the class because of athletic achievements. Because my friend chose to confront the teacher directly instead of going to the principal, the teacher acknowledged playing favorites and opted to do what was right. My friend offered to tutor the athletic students in the class as well. Both the teacher and my friend were able to learn from the experience, and they still communicated even after my friend graduated.

SPEAK, SHINE, SPEAK: Shine's integrity manifests as consistent behavior, predictability, and reliability.

ACTION STEP: Breathe... Create a promise journal. Every day, write three promises to yourself. Celebrate the ones you keep! And Breathe...

Today I am going to play with integrity in this way!

Share your play on Twitter, Facebook, Instagram, Google+
Use #shineonbook

Secret #28

SPIRITUALITY

"Spirituality is the unique understanding that there is something in the universe that is greater than yourself."
— Angel Marie

Spirituality

Spirituality is the freedom to connect to, understand, and experience something greater than yourself. It is the search to unlock the meaning of existence. Religion and spirituality can be related, as each creates different avenues to connect to your higher power. Both religion and spirituality offer a boundless knowing, unwavering security, and limitless love, which offer a connection to your higher self. This connection creates a path to inner peace, clarity, and balance. The awareness that thoughts or prayers can build our reality increases our success in life, while the limitless love of a higher power or God can guide us when we are in troubling times.

Coming from a Catholic background, my religious views shifted in college. I participated in many faiths by attending different places of worship. Because of those experiences, I gained an acceptance for all beliefs. I attended Catholic Mass with my mama and Buddhist ceremonies with my friends. I connected with the energy of Mother Nature. I found a spiritual connection that empowers, guides, and protects me. This connection came with no labels or attachments.

Someone close to me experienced molestation as a child. Their spiritual belief system left them feeling ashamed for something they had no control over. As they grew and acquired their own spiritual understanding, they were able to overcome the shame of their experience. Over time, this person found peace and a renewed connection to their own personal power.

SPEAK, SHINE, SPEAK: Shine's spirituality, like that of all creatures, great and small, is closely linked to Mother Earth.

ACTION STEP: Breathe... Take ten minutes every day to meditate or pray about the core values of your religious or spiritual belief system. Write down three ways your spiritual or religious values influence your daily choices. And Breathe...

Today I am going to play with spirituality in this way!

Share your play on Twitter, Facebook, Instagram, Google+
Use #shineonbook

Secret #29

HONESTY

"Honesty is a limitless gift to your character."
— Angel Marie

Honesty

Honesty is a combination of respect and integrity. It is about being fair and telling the truth. It involves speaking and listening from your heart. Recognizing this trait in others comes from having an awareness of your own honesty. Honesty is a gift we give ourselves because it creates positive relationships. When you are honest with yourself, you respect yourself. When you are honest with others, others trust you.

In grammar school, I went to a store with a group of friends. I saw someone else stealing, so I stole a toy, too. I felt dishonest and worried about getting caught. At home, my mama asked me about the toy. I confessed, and she took me to return it. I felt shame at getting caught, yet being honest with my mama and the store helped me feel relief.

A college student and friend follows several celebrities on social media. He was excited to volunteer for one of his idols at ComiCon. After following specific instructions from the celebrity to set up the stage, he overheard him telling another volunteer that it was all wrong and to change it. That experience was a valuable lesson in discernment concerning another person's honesty.

Social media has a way of catching us in little white lies. A friend was caught in a lie on social media after turning down a volunteer obligation, saying she had a family obligation. Yet her picture was tagged on social media at a party. She was busted. We discussed how in the future she could politely decline rather than make up a story.

SPEAK, SHINE, SPEAK: Shine's honesty comes from pure love and her inability to lie.

ACTION STEP: Breathe... When you put your shoes on for the day, say, "Today, I walk with honesty." And Breathe...

Today I am going to play with honesty in this way!

_____
_____
_____
_____
_____
_____
_____
_____

Share your play on Twitter, Facebook, Instagram, Google+
Use #shineonbook

Secret #30

MANIFESTING

"Manifesting is creating your whole life as an awesome adventure."
— Angel Marie

Manifesting

Manifesting is using thoughts, imagination, and words to create the life you want. Manifesting is an art, a magnetic attractor that draws people with similar thoughts and feelings together. You bring into your life images you visualize or words you repeat in your mind. Manifesting is like ordering online. You state your desire by your keystrokes. When you have a thought and take action to support it, positive results are created.

A friend shared how she manifested the partner, the house, and lifestyle of her dreams. Using visualizations, affirmations, and imagination, she created her magical life. She thought about the kind of partner she wanted to meet and the neighborhood she wanted to live in. She visited that neighborhood, ate at local restaurants, and went grocery shopping in the area. Months later, at the grocery store, she met a man who lived up the street. After a few dates, she visited his house and was astounded to discover it looked exactly like the one she envisioned.

After an accident that totaled my car, I put manifesting to work for me. Outside, I closed my eyes and visualized my new car in the empty parking space. I could see the color, make, and model of my awesome new car. I said out loud, "The process will be easy." That afternoon, I found exactly what I was looking for, and it was in my price range. I bought it the same day!

SPEAK, SHINE, SPEAK: Shine manifests by intuitively sending messages to me. She intensely stares at me until I focus on her and understand what she is communicating.

ACTION STEP: Breathe... Design a manifestation poster. Attach pictures or words of your desires. Post it where you can see it. While staring at it, visualize your dreams. And Breathe...

Today I am going to play with manifesting in this way!

Share your play on Twitter, Facebook, Instagram, Google+
Use #shineonbook

Secret #31

PASSION/ PURPOSE

*"To play with passion
is to have an enthusiastic purpose."*
— Angel Marie

Passion/Purpose

Your purpose is a burning inside of you that feels so good it creates the passion to act. Passion is the enthusiasm to take action. Purpose is the reason you do what you do. Your passions guide you as you discover your purpose. When you share your passion and purpose with others, you bring more joy to others, and create higher self-esteem and greater self-worth. Combining your passion and purpose helps you achieve a more balanced and successful life!

Learning something new can connect you to an undiscovered passion. After a speaking event, a woman came to me looking for ways to feel better and improve her health. We talked about how different foods could help with her mood and energy. Months later, she contacted me to say she was feeling better and had been studying more about nutrition. She found the information fascinating and chose to take classes to become a nutritionist. I was excited that she found her purpose in an unexpected way.

It is easy for me to be passionate about things, because I will try anything once. I love being energetic and sharing this energy with others. My purpose is being a catalyst for joy!

SPEAK, SHINE, SPEAK: Shine is amazingly passionate! It is funny to watch her staring at her squeaky ball. She is so focused on that toy, as well as her desire for me to throw it. To Shine, that ball is her whole world for that moment. She knows she wants something and is willing to stare it down until it happens. That is a very serious passion and purpose.

ACTION STEP: Breathe... Once a week, sit with a trusted friend, coach, or family member. Brainstorm one idea to better understand your passion. Write one action to perform each week. And Breathe...

Today, I am going to play with passion and purpose in this way!

Share your play on Twitter, Facebook, Instagram, Google+
Use #shineonbook

Secret #32

SHAME/ EMBARRASSMENT

"Understanding the lessons of shame and embarrassment allows us to Shine brighter."
— Angel Marie

Shame/Embarrassment

Shame and embarrassment are illusions created by our beliefs. Shame can also be created by fear of others' reactions. By living in the moment, we can move on. When we feel shame, we usually have a lesson to learn about ourselves. We create a shame mentality when we cling to the feeling of shame even after we understand the lesson. Shame does not define you, and embarrassing situations can, in time, become a huge giggle. Overcoming moments of shame and embarrassment builds self-esteem and confidence.

Even today, I feel shame about my learning disability. When working with a friend on a flyer for a speaking event, I spelled a word wrong. I was embarrassed when my friend laughed. I had to take a moment to let go of the initial feeling of hurt. I allowed myself to be vulnerable and explained that laughing at my dyslexia was an uncomfortable trigger. Her understanding of how hurt I felt deepened our friendship. At the same time, by having spoken up for myself, I increased my personal power.

A young client came in mortified that her mother posted a baby picture on social media on her birthday. We talked about how her mother had done this out of love, and that her embarrassment came from fear of the judgment of her peers. To overcome her embarrassment, she turned the situation into a positive and commented on how cute she looked.

SPEAK, SHINE, SPEAK: Even Shine shows shame when I catch her in the trash can, yet a minute later she wants to play. By living in the moment, Shine is able to move on quickly and enjoy life.

ACTION STEP: Breathe... Write down an embarrassing moment. Read it out loud until you can laugh at it. And Breathe...

Today I am going to play with shame/embarrassment in this way!

_____
_____
_____
_____
_____
_____
_____
_____

Share your play on Twitter, Facebook, Instagram, Google+
Use #shineonbook

Secret #33

APPRECIATION/ GRATITUDE

"The feeling of gratitude and appreciation can leave you breathless."
— Angel Marie

Appreciation/Gratitude

Appreciation is experiencing the value of others as well as your own value. Gratitude is the action that expresses your appreciation. We all experience and express gratitude in our own unique ways; taking the time to understand one another is mutual appreciation. Sharing small moments of gratitude can help you feel more inspired, energized, and empowered.

My BFF, Nancy, shows enormous appreciation for people and always wants them to feel important. She is abundantly giving and helpful, and she always goes the extra mile to help her friends feel loved. One of the true gifts she shared with me is how she says, "You deserve all the happiness you receive."

A fourteen-year-old student lived with a loving family, yet she did not feel valued. I asked her what actions her parents could take to show her their appreciation. She replied, "I don't know." We worked to create a list of ways that would make her feel that her family supported her, such as attending school functions and encouraging her creative activities. By recognizing what appreciation meant to her, and expressing that to loved ones, she discovered her family was happy to give her the appreciation she sought.

When I was a kid, birthdays were all about appreciation and love. My mama would post signs all over the house that said, "Happy Birthday, Baby." I loved this practice so much that I adopted it in my own life. When I visit a friend, I leave notes of gratitude around the house or in jacket pockets. This playful act demonstrates my appreciation for the people in my life.

SPEAK, SHINE, SPEAK: Shine shows appreciation and gratitude with her kisses and cuddling.

ACTION STEP: Breathe... Once a week, send a handwritten thank you letter, and clearly state your appreciation for an act of kindness. And Breathe...

Today I am going to play with appreciation/gratitude in this way!

Share your play on Twitter, Facebook, Instagram, Google+
Use #shineonbook

Secret #34

NUTRITION

*"To nourish your body
is an opportunity to honor yourself."*
— Angel Marie

Nutrition

Good nutrition is necessary for exceptional growth and health. Where and when you eat is part of nutrition, too. When we use proper fuel for a car, it runs more efficiently. It is the same for your body. Information on good nutrition is available in many places, yet we often choose to ignore it. Eating for nutrition is eating for color (red, dark green, and orange) and for what's in season. Good nutrition allows you to maintain your physical well-being, which builds self-esteem and confidence.

When I eat, I create a calm environment without distractions from the phone, television, or computer. This allows my body to digest food in peace. To support my metabolism, I put my favorite titanium spork down between each bite, breathe, and appreciate my meal.

A coaching client was having trouble reaching her ideal weight. As we talked, it became apparent that she had an unhealthy obsession with food. We talked about reading serving sizes and nutrition facts on everything she enjoyed eating. When she came back, she shared with me that she had started eating only the recommended serving size and buying healthier alternatives. She was shocked at how this small step greatly affected her weight and success with her health.

SPEAK, SHINE, SPEAK: Animals will not eat something they sense is not good for them. Shine loves celery. Yet, on one occasion, I bought non-organic celery. Shine left it on the floor and refused to eat it!

ACTION STEP: Breathe... Prepare a nutritious snack before you leave the house each day. Include raw vegetables, fruits, or nuts. And Breathe...

Today I am going to play with nutrition in this way!

Share your play on Twitter, Facebook, Instagram, Google+
Use #shineonbook

Secret #35

MISSION/GOALS

*"Embrace your mission
to create your amazing life."*
— Angel Marie

Mission/Goals

Setting goals is seeing success over failure. Be specific in your mission; it can be emotional, material, or physical. Creating a mission helps you achieve your goals both personally and professionally. Goals are promises you make to yourself. Missions are acts you undertake to reach them. Keeping to your mission is empowering. Share your mission! Create a network that will hold you accountable for your goals.

At a retreat for high school students, we discussed the importance of goals. By the end of the session, students understood the value of making promises to themselves. It was exciting to hear the amazing ways they chose to engage their personal missions when answering questions about their passions and their impact on the world.

I am always inspired to help. This book is one way to share my story to motivate others. Some days my dyslexia caused me to get stuck on a single sentence, or made the words on the page seem to move around, yet I committed twenty hours a week to writing in order to make my vision a reality. A team of coaches helped me with wellness, marketing, and writing, allowing me to see this mission to completion.

Social media is a great place to create a network of accountability for your goals. My hair artist, Ms. Donna, joined a group to develop skills for healthy eating. The group shared exercises, grocery lists, and meal prep ideas. They also had a forum for success stories, support, and motivation from others with common goals.

Ms. Donna said this kept her excited and empowered to improve her lifestyle.

SPEAK, SHINE, SPEAK: Shine's unconditional love and companionship complements my life and demonstrates her mission to be a great companion dog.

ACTION STEP: Breathe... Join with a group of trusted friends and create a thirty-day challenge to reach together. Hold each other accountable, and celebrate your victories. And Breathe...

Today I am going to play with mission/goals in this way!

_____
_____
_____
_____
_____
_____
_____
_____

Share your play on Twitter, Facebook, Instagram, Google+
Use #shineonbook

Secret #36

CONFIDENCE

"Don't let anyone dim your Shine!"

— Angel Marie

Confidence

Confidence is connected to your power, strengths, and ability to succeed. The only person that can deem you worthy or unworthy is you. A lack of confidence creates guilt, sadness, and disconnectedness. Feeling good about yourself and what you do causes others to feel good around you. Confidence builds personal power and self-esteem.

My story encouraged one woman to change her mental game. She made adjustments to boost confidence. She read uplifting books, watched motivational videos, and attended life-affirming workshops. By standing taller with her shoulders back, her body language said, "I am confident." This posture changed how she felt about herself. On social media, she enthusiastically shared about all the new people she was meeting and the new activities she was engaging in.

During dance classes, my mama told her students to keep their heads up and smile. This taught me very early on that posture was a valuable part of confidence. Part of why everyone says I am always happy is because I am aware of my self-image and how I present myself. Even on days when I have low energy, I choose to walk with my head up and a big smile on my face, which helps me feel better and have a great day.

SPEAK, SHINE, SPEAK: Shine receives clear commands from me, so she knows what will happen next in her daily routine. This gives her confidence and helps her feel relaxed in all situations.

ACTION STEP: Breathe… At every red light, sit up, take a deep breath, and say out loud, "I approve of myself and love myself deeply and completely." And Breathe…

Today I am going to play with confidence in this way!

Share your play on Twitter, Facebook, Instagram, Google+
Use #shineonbook

Secret #37

LISTENING

"Breathe in silence and create a positive inner space so that others will love to speak to you."
— Angel Marie

Listening

Practicing active listening is a process of relaxing, focusing on the speaker, and maintaining appropriate eye contact. When you listen, you use all the senses and maintain an awareness of both verbal and nonverbal messages. We all have different styles of speaking.

Good listening is focusing on what is being said, rather than on the delivery of how something is said. Improving your listening skills benefits your relationships and increases productivity in your academic and professional life.

When I was a kid, I had a stutter. I had low self-esteem, so my sister Janine would "help" me finish my sentences. After a while, she just spoke for me. A tutor explained that stuttering was a symptom of my dyslexia. When others would interrupt, my brain would have to start all over again. When I was allowed the time to think before I spoke, I was able to share my ideas and feel more confident.

A parent shared how she shifted her speaking and listening by asking open-ended questions and noticing body language. If someone crossed their arms while she was speaking to them, she knew this person was not open to her message. She would clarify her understanding by saying, "This is what I heard you say." These changes in communication made positive waves in her relationships with friends and co-workers.

SPEAK, SHINE, SPEAK: Shine's trainer, Lisa, says Shine understands tones and emotions. She recognizes visual cues, such as body language, and connects that to a verbal command. Because Shine is a herding dog, she is always scanning her surroundings and using all her senses to listen to the world around her.

ACTION STEP: Breathe... When talking to others, repeat back to them the key points you heard them say. And Breathe...

Today I am going to play with listening in this way!

Share your play on Twitter, Facebook, Instagram, Google+
Use #shineonbook

Secret #38

FEAR

"Overcoming your greatest fear creates limitless growth."
— Angel Marie

Fear

Fear is imagining a perceived negative outcome. Fears are meant to protect us from injury or death, yet the "unknown" can be more frightening. The energy that comes from feeling fear stops us from taking positive action. When we accept "fear fantasy" as reality, we experience anxiety and stress. To understand your fear, identify it, embrace it, breathe into it, release it, and move on.

A high school athlete broke his arm. He had been an all-star football player. He feared he had nothing left. He felt abandoned by his friends because they were busy practicing. We talked about how his injury was only temporary. By cheering from the sidelines and hanging out after practice, he was able to stay connected with his teammates. By releasing his fear of rejection, he was able to heal faster and recreate his self-esteem.

When I started my first business, I had as much fear of success as I did of failure. If I did succeed, I wondered if I would be good enough to continue and grow. I also wondered if this was really what I wanted to do for the rest of my life. When I identified this fear, I realized it was an illusion. I recognized I could choose to move on at any time and create another business. This realization made me feel powerful.

SPEAK, SHINE, SPEAK: Shine may be cautious in unfamiliar situations, yet I have never seen Shine fearful. One of the reasons Shine is fearless is because of her great disposition and continual socialization.

ACTION STEP: Breathe... Identify your fear and say, "I am safe to move past my fear of _____." Write down a positive action to move past this fear. Repeat as needed. And Breathe...

Today I am going to play with getting out of fear in this way!

Share your play on Twitter, Facebook, Instagram, Google+
Use #shineonbook

Secret #39

PLAY

"Exercise your playful spirit and Shine On!"

— Angel Marie

Play

Play is just plain fun! Play is an experience that brings joy and raises energy. Play is a process. Play is as important as structure. Children have so much energy because they recharge with play. Parents need play, too! We learn teamwork and leadership through games and sports. Play is a feel-good energy boost that creates a shift in mood and productivity. Making the conscious choice to look for opportunities to play creates more self-esteem and success in life.

A participant at a lunch-and-learn event had so much fun that he was excited to bring play into his work and personal life. He shared that he wanted to laugh more and experience more joy. When he saw me again at his company's corporate picnic, he ran up to me and said with enthusiasm, "Wow! I love my life because I put more play into it!"

My hair artist, Ms. Donna, and I make it a playful event when she does my hair. We share positive stories over dinner before the haircut begins. Afterwards, we go to our local ice cream shop where everyone knows us. Sometimes we finish the evening with a walk or a swim with Shine.

Wherever I go, "play energy" follows me, because I have a positive and enthusiastic attitude. I consciously choose to make play a priority because it is my passion. I share this energy with others by smiling, laughing, and sharing entertaining stories.

SPEAK, SHINE, SPEAK: Play is Shine's purpose, too! Play gives Shine true fulfillment and joy in her life. When Shine and I play catch, she is always smiling and fully engaged.

ACTION STEP: Breathe... Before leaving the house in the morning, stop, stand in place, spin around and say, "Shine On!" three times. And Breathe...

Today I am going to play with play in this way!

Share your play on Twitter, Facebook, Instagram, Google+
Use #shineonbook

Secret #40

ADVERSITY

"*Adversity is a source of powerful growth and steadfast resolve.*"
— Angel Marie

Adversity

Adversity is the person, situation, or limitation that stops us like a net. It feels like a wall or blockage we experience when working toward something. Adversity causes us to feel like nothing is working, or that quitting is the only option. Seeing adversity in a different light allows things to fall into place and flow. The key is to experience situations without judgment. Asking others for guidance or another perspective can be helpful. To be unshakable even in moments of uncertainty is to conquer self-doubt. Determination and tenacity come from overcoming adversity.

I always find a way to complete challenges that I meet, even if the way I fulfill the task is different than others. When I bought my first phone in 1990, it was a challenge for me to follow directions because the instructions involved words. It was the same in 2005 when I bought a smart phone. However, this time I was able to attend classes, watch videos, and ask questions until I learned how to use my new device.

The pressures of school, work, and relationships can be stressful for anyone. A college student shared with me that the adversity of balancing homework and hours at work was straining her personal life. By creating a schedule for better time management and communicating her needs with family and friends, she was able to maintain a more balanced and harmonious life.

SPEAK, SHINE, SPEAK: Shine does not experience adversity because, in her mind, everything is a game. She has so much energy and determination to figure things out.

ACTION STEP: Breathe... Identify a challenge. Say out loud, "I accept this challenge, and it is resolved easily and quickly!" And Breathe...

Today I am going to play with moving through adversity in this way!

Share your play on Twitter, Facebook, Instagram, Google+
Use #shineonbook

Secret #41

SELF-TALK

"Positive self-talk is your personal cheerleader."

— Angel Marie

Self-Talk

Self-talk is chatter inside your mind that can either be a pep talk or a real downer. Positive self-talk boosts confidence and self-esteem, while internal nagging, negativity, and criticism can sabotage success. Your inner conversation influences behavior, attitudes, habits, and relationships. Listen carefully to your inner self-talk. Practicing moments to pause, delete, or change thoughts that are not helpful can build self-esteem and create greater success.

I practice positive self-talk by looking at life situations as challenges rather than adversity. If I feel frustrated or want to quit, I use self-talk to build strength, clarity, and endurance. I speak out loud, using my first and middle name to ask questions or say uplifting affirmations such as, "Angel Marie, you Shine, and everything is easy." I do this with such enthusiasm that Shine gets excited! She is my cheerleader and energy booster!

A webinar participant's self-talk was negative and self-deprecating. We talked about how this behavior can hold him back, cause stress, and contribute to health problems. He committed to speaking to himself in the same way he would to a dear friend. He even came up with a great system. Instead of "can't," he would say "don't." The word "can't" creates a mentality of permanence. Saying "don't" connects you to your personal success. "I can't eat dessert" versus "I don't want to eat dessert" is a powerful shift!

SPEAK, SHINE, SPEAK: Shine has wonderful energy all the time because her self-talk is extremely childlike and positive.

ACTION STEP: Breathe... Every time you look in a mirror, say your first and middle name out loud, and state a positive affirmation. A great example is: "[Your name]! You are brilliant!" Do this three times. And Breathe...

Today I am going to play with self-talk in this way!

Share your play on Twitter, Facebook, Instagram, Google+
Use #shineonbook

Secret #42

ABUNDANCE

*"Personal abundance comes
from fulfilling your unique desires."*
— Angel Marie

Abundance

Abundance is different for everyone, yet at its core, it means "plenty." Most people think of their monetary value, career position, and personal status when explaining their abundance. However, abundance can also refer to great health, personal success, or even the number of friends you have.

Defining what abundance means to you helps you gain greater clarity, so you can focus on the things you really want to create. This is how you amplify your personal power. When you feel abundant, you experience more gratitude. As you experience more gratitude, you receive more abundance.

A mom contacted me because she was excited about how much abundance she had in her life. She shared that by giving herself permission to be abundant instead of settling for less, she found more opportunities and self-confidence.

I feel abundant because I have cultivated many relationships built on mutual respect, trust, and support. I have an abundance of people whom I love and who love me. I feel secure because I have so many friends to turn to when I am looking for advice. I can call Shine's trainer and friend, Lisa, if I have a question about Shine. I call my mama for unconditional love. My BFF, Nancy, is always there to offer support and motivation. In turn, I give abundantly to my friends, family, social media connections, and others.

SPEAK, SHINE, SPEAK: In Shine's reality, life is good because she always has the food and water she needs. She also has toys to play with and someone to love her. In her mind, this is an abundant life.

ACTION STEP: Breathe… Write down three things that you desire. Visualize, play, and focus on these things for five minutes each day. And Breathe …

Today I am going to play with abundance in this way!

Share your play on Twitter, Facebook, Instagram, Google+
Use #shineonbook

Secret #43

AHA MOMENT

"Aha moments expand our reality."
— Angel Marie

Aha Moment

Aha moments are flashes of insights or inspired realizations that are unique and deeply personal. They are moments of clarity when you gain real wisdom that can be used to change your life. For example, you think a friend is hiding something from you. Then you find out they really had your back. Aha moments are more than a lesson you learn from that experience. They are shifts in your understanding of the way you think about things. Aha moments can sometimes be felt as a whole body sensation, like goosebumps.

A young adult on social media was afraid to comment about his support of gay marriage because he felt others would respond negatively. When he finally posted his support, he was surprised by all the positive comments. He realized he could be his authentic self without fear of judgment. This aha moment increased his self-esteem.

My learning disability gave me the opportunity to experience amazing aha moments. To help me with learning my alphabet, my mama showed me how to recognize letters by placing sandpaper cutouts in a shoebox. The texture of the paper helped me remember the pattern of the letters. My aha moment was that I could learn anything when I turned it into play.

SPEAK, SHINE, SPEAK: When I first took Shine home to our two-story condo, she was confused and afraid of stairs. It took a lot of coaxing for her to learn about them. Shine's aha moment was discovering that it was safe for her to climb the stairs.

ACTION STEP: Breathe... When you take a shower, take a dry erase marker or soap crayon to write down ideas that come to you. And Breathe...

Today I am going to play with aha moments in this way!

Share your play on Twitter, Facebook, Instagram, Google+
Use #shineonbook

Secret #44

TRUST

"The secret to building trust is to be honest and patient with others."
— Angel Marie

Trust

Trust is believing in yourself and others. To trust is to have confidence in your choices. People who trust rely on strengths, abilities, or character—their own and others'. Trust involves a positive outlook about a situation or maintaining faith that things will work out. Trust is believing intuition and following through with your actions. The feeling of trust takes great integrity and honor to build. When trust is present, your personal power and self-esteem shine.

In fifth grade, I was in gymnastics. I also participated in ballet and tap recitals with my mama's dance classes. I told my mama that I wanted to combine dance and acrobatics for an upcoming talent show. We put our heads together and believed in each other's talents to create a routine. I trusted myself to be able to perform something unique in front of the whole school. Trusting myself and my mama, I succeeded in being a finalist in the talent show.

A mom shared her doubts about taking the next step in a relationship. She had been dating her partner for several months and wanted to introduce him to her children. We talked about how she should trust her intuition, as well as the feelings of love and respect her partner had for her. After a wonderful day at the park with her children and partner, she called to share her relief and joy.

SPEAK, SHINE, SPEAK: Shine trusts me as her companion to feed her and care for her. Animals, in general, trust in the process of life.

ACTION STEP: Breathe... Make a commitment to yourself to go to bed at the same time every night. Keep this promise to yourself to develop self-trust. And Breathe...

Today I am going to play with trust in this way!

Share your play on Twitter, Facebook, Instagram, Google+
Use #shineonbook

Secret #45

JUDGMENT

*"Feel your inner Shine
and never judge another."*
— Angel Marie

Judgment

Judgments come from society, religion, culture, or media. Judgment is perception based on individual learning and understanding of reality. For example, you might judge someone who wears clothes that are different than yours. It doesn't mean your clothes are better or worse. It is just a perception.

Judgments can help create boundaries and keep us safe. How we act on our judgments can affect our success personally and professionally.

I posted one of my services on social media. Someone I did not know left a negative comment. Instead of commenting back, I messaged friends to share something positive on that post. They responded with uplifting messages without bringing the other person down. Eventually, the negative commenter removed his post.

When I was little, I would come home crying because of judgments from others. I was judged because of my athletic build and the way I dressed. My sister, Janine, would yell at people for saying I looked like a boy. I realized I had no desire to conform to the cookie-cutter ideal for a girl. My dad encouraged me to be the athletic and unique person I am. He said that if people could not see my beauty, they were missing out.

In my adult life, I have chosen not to conform to societal expectations of beauty. I leave my hair white because that is my authentic self. Because I am not controlled by the judgments of others, I am free to break away from society's expectations.

SPEAK, SHINE, SPEAK: Shine's judgment is based on positive and negative reinforcement. Her understanding of the world is very simple.

ACTION STEP: Breathe… Before getting out of the car, take three minutes to breathe and say, "I release any judgments on myself or others." And Breathe …

Today I am going to play with letting go of judgment in this way!

Share your play on Twitter, Facebook, Instagram, Google+
Use #shineonbook

Secret #46

IMAGINATION/ CREATIVITY

"Shine with creativity, imagination, and wonder!"
— Angel Marie

Imagination/Creativity

Imagination is the ability to come up with concepts and ideas. Creativity involves taking steps to achieve your ideas. Creativity and imagination connect us to our authenticity and personal vision of success.

A client shared that she felt uncreative and limited by boring tasks and responsibilities. Looking at her life, we discovered that she actually did possess an element of creativity in doing her daily tasks. At school, she had a creative way of using highlighters in notes. She also used her imagination to visualize her day every morning on her way to school. By recognizing these moments of creativity and imagination, she became more productive and enthusiastic about her life.

A fellow speaker at a retreat wore interesting clothes and dyed her hair different colors. She explained that she had loved to wear unique styles as a kid, so she chose to study fashion in college. Her creativity allowed her authentic self to shine, and it helped her find her perfect career as an alternative fashion designer.

We live in a time when it is easy to share our unique gifts with the world. Social media has given us the freedom to unleash our imaginations. I have seen so much creativity on social media! In particular, on YouTube, so many people—including me!—can share tips and insights on personal successes and creative projects.

SPEAK, SHINE, SPEAK: I love to watch Shine tap into her creativity when playing with treat puzzles. She uses her nose and paws to figure out how to get to the goodies inside!

ACTION STEP: Breathe… Every day before breakfast, write down one imaginative idea and one action step to manifest it into reality. And Breathe …

Today I am going to play with creativity and imagination in this way!

Share your play on Twitter, Facebook, Instagram, Google+
Use #shineonbook

Secret #47

HONORING/ RESPECT

"When you respect yourself, you shine with honor!"
— Angel Marie

Honoring/Respect

Honoring is a deep level of respect created by the perception of a person, situation, or group. A part of honoring is the desire to experience the qualities we find important and valuable in others. Honoring is understanding that every person has unique value. We honor others and ourselves through praise, listening, and respecting boundaries. Respecting others also honors who we are. A person who is honest and respectful of others is perceived as honorable.

I honor all my coaches and teachers because of the knowledge they have shared. Because of their insight, I have learned new ways to care for my health, businesses, and spirit.

One of the ways I play with honor is that I write notes to myself and hide them around the house. I love finding these notes because they create positive energy. Another way I respect myself is to keep my environment clean and safe. I make my bed every morning and clean all the dishes before going to bed at night. By doing these things, I feel empowered and grateful.

A student felt depressed and unhappy about herself and her life. We discussed that she was not doing things to honor herself. Instead, she spent too much time giving to others. We talked about ways she could do more to nurture her spirit, such as buying flowers for herself and enjoying more moments alone. By respecting herself, she felt more balanced and empowered. She could feel her self-esteem rising.

SPEAK, SHINE, SPEAK: Shine honors herself by taking time to rest and play!

ACTION STEP: Breathe... Once a week, buy a small gift that you can display as a personal reminder to honor yourself and put yourself first. And Breathe...

Today I am going to play with honoring and respect in this way!

Share your play on Twitter, Facebook, Instagram, Google+
Use #shineonbook

Secret #48

CLARITY/PEACE

"When you have inner peace, clarity comes naturally."
— Angel Marie

Clarity/Peace

Clarity is the ability to perceive and understand in a balanced way. Peace is when we experience a state of harmony within ourselves. With peace comes the ability to agree to disagree without judgment. Clarity is having inner peace no matter what is going on around you. Clarity and peace are a conscious choice you can make daily. When you have clarity, you feel more confident, focused, and energetic.

A workshop participant shared that she felt scattered and frustrated. We discussed the ways this lack of peace was affecting her life. Using breathing techniques and visualization tools, she calmed her mind and emotions. She did this daily before going to school and work. She reported back that she felt more inspired and focused.

I'm a Gemini, so I can multitask with the best of them. I taught myself to address one lesson or homework assignment at a time, and then set it aside. I was blessed to have tutors help me with focus and planning. To overcome a lack of clarity, I set a timer for a half hour. At the bell, I would leave for ten minutes to run around, yell, breathe, or talk to a friend—anything other than look at the homework. I balanced study and play to find peace and clarity in my schoolwork.

SPEAK, SHINE, SPEAK: Companion animals such as Shine connect with the clarity of their person and environment. Unfocused or scattered surroundings cause animals to feel agitated. Shine expresses her agitation by whining and pacing. When Shine and I are on a schedule, she is happy and relaxed.

ACTION STEP: Breathe... Every time you go to the bathroom, take three deep breaths. Leave your phone in another room. And Breathe...

Today I am going to play with clarity and peace in this way!

_____
_____
_____
_____
_____
_____
_____
_____
_____

Share your play on Twitter, Facebook, Instagram, Google+
Use #shineonbook

Secret #49

JOY

*"Your ultimate joy
is in connecting to your Shine!"*
— Angel Marie

Joy

Joy is a delightful state of happiness. It is the ultimate feel-good emotion! Joy is feeling amazing glee and connecting with the awesome, shining version of you. We can experience joy anywhere, anytime. The practice of joy makes everything in life easier and more fun. Give yourself permission to be happy with who you are.

I am often asked how I stay in joy. On social media, at events, and in videos, I am always shining with joy. I feel that joy is a muscle to be exercised. Before going to a party or even the grocery store, I take a few seconds to smile, breathe, and laugh!

One of my fondest childhood memories is waiting for my dad to get home from work to play basketball in our driveway. I waited with so much enthusiasm for this special time with my dad. Even after his passing, this memory brings a huge smile to my face.

A manager for a large company felt she lacked happiness in her life. She missed the joyful feeling she used to get when finishing a project or going to an event. Using simple tips, such as taking time to smile and giving herself a pep talk before going to a meeting, she found herself enjoying the moment again. Using this self-talk, she created joy in any situation.

SPEAK, SHINE, SPEAK: I love when Shine is in joy while playing ball or swimming. Her trainer, Lisa, says that dogs feel the most joy when their companions come home. When Shine is excited to see me, her tail wags so fast she falls over and howls with joy.

ACTION STEP: Breathe... At every red light, laugh out loud at least three times. And Breathe...

Today I am going to play with joy in this way!

Share your play on Twitter, Facebook, Instagram, Google+
Use #shineonbook

Secret #50

CHANGE/ TRANSFORMATION

*"Every new moment
is a chance to shift your reality."*
— Angel Marie

Change/Transformation

Change is constant. We are all hardwired to want to learn and grow. We celebrate positive transformations with milestones such as birthdays, anniversaries, and graduations. Some life transformations are outside of our control. Moving, changing schools, or getting a new job are examples of major changes we all experience at one time or another. Boredom helps us recognize a desire for change. Sometimes events that seem terrible can set you on an amazing adventure. By flowing with and adapting to change, you can increase your personal power and raise your self-esteem.

During a relationship change, it is important to have a support system and positive coping techniques. Many students find a school counselor or coach to be a great resource.

In high school, my mama and stepdad were planning to move to California. Because I made the varsity softball team my freshman year, I wanted to stay in Arizona. When a misunderstanding caused me to be removed from the team, I chose to move to California. This transition was one of the best things to ever happen to me, even though I didn't think so at the time. My new high school had one of the best softball teams in the state. I also met a fabulous student counselor who helped me during my parents' divorce.

SPEAK, SHINE, SPEAK: Change can be difficult for animals, too. Even small changes that you make in your own life can be huge for an animal. My sleep schedule and daily activities can affect

Shine. If I am not getting enough sleep or taking time to rest, Shine may not be rested either.

ACTION STEP: Breathe... Today, transform your thinking. Instead of saying, "I can't," say, "I am." Example: "I can't read" becomes "I am reading." And Breathe...

Today I am going to play with change and transformation in this way!

Share your play on Twitter, Facebook, Instagram, Google+
Use #shineonbook

Secret #51

AUTHENTICITY

*"What is honest, heartfelt,
and brings you joy is your authentic self."*
— Angel Marie

Authenticity

Authenticity is accepting, believing in, and being true to yourself. It is understanding diversity, in that you are a unique and original being. Authenticity is not relying on the opinions or beliefs of others to create your true personality, spirit, or character. To be the best version of yourself is to look in the mirror and totally accept what you see. When we change to fit others' perceptions, we block our true selves. Authenticity creates more success, self-confidence, and joy!

In grammar school, my mama wanted me to dress well. I would wear shorts underneath my dresses and hide a T-shirt to change into on the way to school. I got busted on picture day in a wrinkly old T-shirt and shorts that didn't match. Mama was not happy, yet that picture captured my authentic self.

During a meeting, another one of my besties, Christina, took me aside and said that I seemed off. I explained that my shoes were not comfortable, and I didn't feel like myself. She smiled and said, "Wear what you want! It's not about your shoes!" The next day I bought seven pairs of tennis shoes in different colors. Now, when I attend a speaking event, I am comfortable and people love my sparkly tennis shoes.

SPEAK, SHINE, SPEAK: Shine is always her true self because she lives in the moment. When I am on the computer, Shine will lie on her back with her legs all splayed out and release a deep breath. I love that she is so relaxed and free to just be herself.

ACTION STEP: Breathe... When choosing your clothing for the day, say at least three times out loud, "I accept my uniqueness and embrace my inner truth!" And Breathe...

Today I am going to play with authenticity in this way!

Share your play on Twitter, Facebook, Instagram, Google+
Use #shineonbook

Secret #52

DIVERSITY

"Shine On! with accepting and appreciating diversity!"
— Angel Marie

Diversity

Race, gender, sexual orientation, and religion are expressions of the diversity in the world. Appreciating and honoring differences is diversity. By acknowledging diversity without judgment, we are all able to be our authentic selves.

One of my BFFs, who is white, is dating a black man. She has many stories about how they've been judged in public. At a restaurant, even today, they get sidelong glances. Her first reaction is anger, and then she feels disappointment because so many people are still judgmental. She is grateful that her family and the people she loves are open to diverse relationships and accepting of her relationship.

One of my most empowering moments in accepting my own diversity occurred at The National March on Washington for Lesbian and Gay Rights. Prior to this event, I had been kicked out of my apartment building because of my sexual orientation. I felt as though I was wearing a bag over my head to hide my identity everywhere I went. Because of my business and my concern that I would lose clients, I really was planning to wear a bag over my head as I set out to join the march. As I stepped off the subway and into that crowd of like-minded individuals, a feeling of pride and solidarity overwhelmed me. Today, I no longer hide my identity, yet I do not feel the need to advocate in anger either. My family loves me for who I am, and my dear friends are proud to know me.

SPEAK, SHINE, SPEAK: Shine loves everyone equally. Especially if they have a treat!

ACTION STEP: Breathe... Once a week for fifteen minutes, choose a culture different than your own and learn about it. Google it, watch a video, or go to the library. And Breathe...

Today I am going to play with acknowledging and respecting diversity in this way!

Share your play on Twitter, Facebook, Instagram, Google+
Use #shineonbook

BONUS ACTION STEP
FREEDOM

"The secret to freedom is to unleash your authentic self and let your personal power Shine On!"
— Angel Marie

Freedom

Freedom is the power to act, speak, or think with no restrictions. It is being able to choose what is best for you. We all want freedom to make choices—even if we fall on our faces. Freedom is self-determination. It is about ruling our personal choices and conduct. True freedom is in your mind, because no one can tell you what to think or feel. When you believe and act on your freedom, you create limitless success, abundant self-esteem, and infinite joy.

A friend's relationship started out very strong and lasted several years. When the relationship ended, he was devastated. He felt like he couldn't live without his partner. His new reality dawned on him while unpacking at his new house. He discovered a painting he had stopped working on while in the relationship. In that instant, he said, "Oh, my gosh. I am free to take art classes, finish this painting, and just be me."

Owning my own business gives me the freedom to share my passions, live by my own schedule, and travel to interesting places.

When you have freedom, you are unstoppable. As a speaker and coach, I am honored to share the path to freedom with you. May you Shine On! with joy and limitless abundance!

SPEAK, SHINE, SPEAK: Shine runs across the beach, splashes in the water, and barks with joy. She loves her freedom. When I allow her to be free from commands and off her leash, Shine experiences pure joy. We can all benefit from allowing ourselves to be off the leash for a little while.

ACTION STEP: Breathe... For at least twenty minutes a day, allow yourself time to play and do something purely for fun. And Breathe...

Today I am going to play with freedom in this way!

Share your play on Twitter, Facebook, Instagram, Google+
Use #shineonbook

A Personal Thank You!

Congratulations! I am so excited that you have chosen to claim your personal success and raise your self-esteem, boost your personal power, and Shine On! I hope the diverse stories you've read in this book have served to bring more inspiration, joy, and playfulness into your life.

Look back on these action steps in *Shine On!* whenever you are looking for encouragement and insight to get through the challenges or changes that are occurring in your life.

And always remember to Shine On!

Thank you,

Angel Marie & Shine

Acknowledgements

Deepest gratitude to my dad for teaching me that I could claim my personal vision of success and accept myself for who I am. Thank you, Daddy-O!

I am infinitely grateful to my mama for her abundant love, and for her being there for me no matter how ambitious my ideas have been.

To my sister friend and BFF, Nancy, I am so blessed that you trust my choices and celebrate my potential. Thank you!

Thank you, Christina, for being my cheerleader, my bestie, and a voice of honesty and tough love—and for our fun video-making sessions!

Ms. Donna, my hair artist and beautiful BFF, thank you for all the time we spend primping and playing—and for your wonderful hugs!

Lisa, your phenomenal connection to Shine and ability to communicate with unconditional love has made you one of our most trusted friends. I appreciate you, BFF!

To Janine and Danny, I appreciate you both for looking out and standing up for me.

To Kaya, who always takes time from her adventures to encourage me, thank you for sharing your courageous spirit.

Thank you, Jenn, for holding a space charged with love and creativity, and for sharing your writing expertise. You rock!

And to Shine, for being a limitless morale booster and always wanting to take a break to play!

Thank you all for the friendship and amazing photos: Val and Stephanie Westover of Westover Photography, Eleanor Mahoney of Images by Eleanor, Rizalde Sherwood of Studio World Photography, Ron Robertson, and Don Thompson of Don Thompson Photography.

A very special thank you to Gloria, Amy, Terry, Melissa, Sue, Karen, Lea, Annette, Wayne, Justin, Anna, Larry, DJ, students, close friends, and volunteers.

To all my coaches and tutors along the way, thank you for your support and guidance.

A special thank you to you, the readers of *Shine On!* By reading this book, you make the world a better place by raising your own self-esteem and sharing your Shine with others!

All of you will always Shine brightly in my heart!

Shine On!

Special FREE Bonus Gift for You

To help you achieve more success,
there are free bonus resources for you at:

www.FreeGiftFromAngelMarie.com

An in-depth training video
on how you can get your Shine On!

The Ideal Professional Speaker for Your Next Conference or Event!

Any organization that wants to develop their people to become "extraordinary" needs to hire Angel Marie for a keynote and/or workshop training!

To Contact or Book Angel Marie to Speak:

Angel Marie Monachelli
24 W. Camelback Rd., Ste. A-413
Phoenix, AZ 85013
(623)-334-3393
Angel@AngelMarieShines.com
www.AngelMarieShines.com